Simple Witchcraft Series

WICCA

A BEGINNER'S GUIDE TO WITCHCRAFT, SPELLS, RITUALS, AND MAGICK

CASSANDRA LARSEN

First Printing, Jan 2016

ISBN-13: 978-1517622008

ISBN-10: 151762200X

www.larsenbooks.wordpress.com

TABLE OF CONTENTS

WHY I WROTE THIS BOOK

Witchcraft is a subject near and dear to my heart. When I first began my journey into this beautiful, soul fulfilling religion, I remember how confusing and difficult it was. Most of the books I read on Wicca and Witchcraft required expensive tools and lengthy, complex rituals that were difficult to understand or follow.

In this book, simplicity is my goal. I am a firm believer that simple rituals and spells are just as meaningful and effective as complex ones—if not more so—as long as you have the will and desire to enact change in your life.

This book is designed for people like you, who are just beginning to discover this life changing path and desire a clear, concise guide to show them the way to connecting with nature and the Divine without spending hundreds of dollars on expensive tools or manuals.

Wicca: A Beginner's Guide to Witchcraft, Spells, Rituals, and Magick is the book I wish I could have read when I first began practicing. In it, I will share my own simple, yet effective, rituals and spells that anyone can do, regardless of experience or budget.

This guide will teach you the basics of Wiccan beliefs, along with meditation and visualization exercises designed to open your mind and expand your consciousness. You will be introduced to the basic Wiccan tools and discover how to create your own inexpensively, as well as how to purify them for magickal use. You will also learn all about the eight Wiccan sabbats, how to cast a magick circle, and powerful spells and rituals for prosperity, success, love, purification, and banishing bad habits.

By the end of this book, you will have all the necessary skills and knowledge you need to begin practicing Wicca today!

Chapter 1: Basic Beliefs

Not many people understand what the Wiccan religion really encompasses. The word "witch" generally evokes feelings of fear and revulsion; however Wicca is one of the most gentle, accepting religions in the world.

Wicca is an earth-based religion reconstructed from ancient, pre-Christian beliefs and practices that focus on living in harmony with the earth, the natural cycles, and the Divine.

Although beliefs among different traditions of Wicca and Witchcraft vary slightly, most traditions agree upon these basic principles:

The Divine

Contrary to popular belief, Witches do not worship Satan, or even believe in hell or a devil. Satan, hell, and sin are all part of Christianity, not Wicca or Witchcraft. We do not blame our choices or mistakes on some devil or evil being; we believe that we are responsible for our own actions and we take responsibility for our lives and the consequences of our choices.

We do, however, believe in a higher power, which we personify into a male and female entity—the God and Goddess.

The God and Goddess reside in all of nature. The sun is ruled by the God, the moon by the Goddess.

Our relationship to the God and Goddess is deeply personal. They are a warm, comforting presence in our everyday lives, always with us, always loving us. They are in the warmth of the sun's rays, the exhilaration of the blowing wind, the gentle mist of rain on our skin, the steady earth beneath our feet. They are present all around us all the time and we constantly strive to deepen our relationship with Them.

ALL GODS AND GODDESSES ARE ONE

Many Witches and Wiccans believe that all gods are one God and all goddesses one Goddess. By whatever name you call the Divine—Jesus, Mother Mary, Buddha, Allah, Brahman, Shakti, Guanyin, Zeus, Aphrodite, Freya, Brigid—Wiccans believe that they are all actually part of the one God and Goddess; they just represent different aspects of Them.

Because we believe that all gods and goddesses are one, we understand that there is no one true religion or path to Divinity. We respect other people's personal and religious beliefs and wish for them to give us the same respect.

We do not proselytize or try to convert other people to our religion. Everyone has the right to believe what they want and practice whatever feels right and natural to them.

REVERENCE FOR NATURE

Of all the Wiccans and Witches I've met over the years, reverence for nature is the most common reason they say they were drawn to this spiritual path.

Witches have a strong connection to the natural world and its energies. We believe that the Divine is present in the earth, the air, the rain, the sun and the moon. The God and Goddess are all around us and we feel Their presence most strongly in nature.

Have you ever sat outside in the grass, the sun shining down on you from above, the wind gently blowing through your hair? Or maybe you prefer the beach; your feet buried in the warm sand while the oceans waves are crashing against the shore? Have you felt that sense of inner peace, the love and connection that surrounds you in those moments?

That is the God and Goddess. In those moments, you are feeling Their presence, Their Divine essence. You are feeling Their spirit and energy flow through you and connecting to Them on a personal level.

We believe that all of nature is sacred, and must therefore be respected. Like our ancient ancestors, we seek to live in harmony with nature and its cycles. We have a strong connection to the natural world and it is through nature that we commune with the God and Goddess.

THE PENTACLE

The pentacle is often misunderstood and wrongly maligned. It's quite common, even in this day and age, to see it connected to demons and devil-worshippers, when in fact they have nothing to do with one another.

In Witchcraft and Wicca, the five points of the pentacle represent the five natural elements—earth, air, fire, water, and spirit—while the circle surrounding the star represents our connection to nature, the elements, and the Divine. The pentacle and pentagram (which is the five pointed star without the circle) are not symbols of evil or maliciousness, but rather of our spiritual connection to the Divine and the natural world.

RITUALS, SPELLS, AND MAGICK

Like the word 'witch,' the term 'spell' often evokes feelings of unease and fear, conjuring up images of hags casting evil hexes and causing mayhem. But in reality, a spell is nothing more than a ritualized prayer.

Have you ever lit a candle and said a prayer for someone who was unwell or in need of help? If so, then you have cast a spell!

In its simplest form, a spell requires calling upon a higher power (or the natural elements) while performing a ritual designed to raise energy and enact change. Religions all around the world incorporate elements of magick and ritual into their practices.

For example, in Judaism, two candles are lit in a ceremonial fashion to honor the God and welcome in the Sabbath. In many Christian churches, incense and holy water are used for purification and blessing. In Buddhism, the use of statues, candles, incense, and offerings are used as a means to purify one's mind and create a peaceful atmosphere in which to meditate.

Similar practices are used in Wiccan rituals and spells. We believe that every one of us has the ability to enact meaningful change in our lives and the world around us through prayer, ritual, and magick.

This isn't to say, however, that magick will solve all of your problems; magick is an aid we can use, but it should not be used as a crutch or as a replacement for hard work.

THE LAW OF THREE

Witches believe in the karmic law of three: whatever you give out is returned to you threefold. This means that whatever energy you send out into the world (good or bad) is returned to you three times over. This is why Witches always strive to do good and only send out positive energy; if you use magick to hurt someone, that negative energy will rebound on you threefold, either in this life or the next.

AN YOU HARM NONE, DO WHAT YE WILL

Wiccans don't believe in sin the way Judeo-Christian religions do—there is no list of commandants that must be followed, no devil tempting us, no hell where we will burn eternally. There is only one rule with which we live by: 'An you harm none, do what ye will'.

We are responsible for our own actions, good and bad. Our moral philosophy is a simple one; whatever you do comes back to you times three, so always strive to do good and never harm.

We do not harm others, nor manipulate anyone by magickal means. In fact, casting a spell on someone else without their permission—regardless if the spell is intended to help them—constitutes doing harm and is strongly discouraged. Our rituals and spells are only used for bringing about positive change, and if used on someone else's behalf, are done only with their permission.

Despite its negative portrayal in movies and books, Wicca is a gentle, peaceful religion focused on living in harmony with nature and deepening our relationship with the Divine.

CHAPTER 2: MEDITATION AND VISUALIZATION

Meditation and visualization are an extremely important part of a Witch's daily practice, as they are the key elements to creating powerful magick.

Meditation allows you to calm your mind and connect with the Divine. It's also the means through which you alter your consciousness and tap into your own energy and the energies around you.

Visualization is the process of manipulating that energy, turning it into reality in order to enact change on the physical plane.

The techniques and exercises in this chapter are designed to improve your skills and increase the power of your magick. Both meditation and visualization take time and practice to master, so don't be discouraged if these seem difficult at first. The following sections will help guide you on your journey.

SIMPLE MEDITATION

Choose a comfortable sitting position, either in a chair or on the ground, somewhere you won't be distracted. Silence your phone, turn off the TV, close your door and tell others you don't wish to be disturbed. If there are distracting noises around you, you can play calm, soothing music to help drown them out until you become skilled enough to block out distractions on your own.

Close your eyes and focus on your breath. Breathing is a very important part of meditation and a main element in altering your state of consciousness.

Slowly inhale to a count of five, expanding your chest and diaphragm as wide as you can. (The diaphragm is the large muscle found at the bottom of your ribcage). If you wish, you can place one hand just below your ribcage. As you inhale, you should feel this area press out against your hand.

When your lungs and diaphragm are as full as you can make them, slowly exhale, again to a count of five. Force as much air out of your lungs, contracting your diaphragm as you do.

Repeat this for several cycles, slowly decreasing your heart rate and releasing all tension from your body.

After a few minutes you should start to feel relaxed and calm. Try to empty your mind of all thoughts, focusing only on your breath. If this is difficult, then choose an image, word, or phrase to focus on, blocking out all other distractions.

This is a great time to relax, releasing any tensions or worries that have been bothering you. Open your consciousness, allowing peace and tranquility to enter your body and mind.

Meditation is an important tool for deepening your relationship with the God and Goddess. Talk to Them if you wish, open yourself up to Their presence.

This is also a great way to release any anger, stress or negativity as well as calm the mind and expand the senses before rituals or magickal workings.

Practice this for at least five minutes each day, slowly increasing the length of your meditation. As the weeks pass, this will become easier and you will find yourself able to enter a relaxed, meditative state almost instantly.

SIMPLE VISUALIZATION

Like meditation, visualization is an important tool for creating successful magick. If you can't visualize the outcome of your spells, you will not be able to send out the energy you need to manifest change.

For this exercise, choose a comfortable sitting position, either in a chair or on the ground. Spend a few minutes breathing and centering yourself. When you are calm and relaxed, close your eyes and picture an object or symbol that is familiar to you. This can be a favorite piece of jewelry, a stylized pentacle, a favorite flower— whatever draws you. When you first start out, you might want to have the object physically present so you can study the details before beginning.

With your eyes closed, visualize this object in as much detail as possible, seeing it as if it is right in front of you.

This will be difficult at first. Your mind may only be able to picture the general shape, losing details the longer you hold it. Other thoughts or images may arise, distracting you. If this happens, simply acknowledge the thought or image, then dismiss it and bring your mind back to your chosen image.

When you are able to hold this image for five minutes without disruption, try visualizing an object you've never seen before. Create it in your mind, adding layers of detail to it until the object seems as real to you as if it were sitting right in front of you.

When you are ready, move on to visualizations of people and places, both familiar and unfamiliar. Add as much detail as you can and try to hold that image for five minutes.

When you have mastered the art of visualization with your eyes closed, then try these techniques with your eyes open.

You will find that this is much more difficult and requires a lot more practice, but it's important for casting a circle and performing spells and rituals.

BREATHING EXERCISE FOR RELEASING NEGATIVITY

Meditation is a great way to relax and relieve stress. The following exercise combines both meditation and visualization to help you relieve stress and banish negativity.

Find a comfortable position and close your eyes. Spend a few minutes focusing on your breath and centering your mind. When ready, visualize a glowing white light surrounding you, pulsing with peace and tranquility.

As you inhale, draw this light into your lungs, allowing it to spread through your body. Feel this light calming you, relaxing your tense muscles.

When you exhale, visualize the stress leaving your body, sinking into the earth below you.

Keep your breath slow and steady. Breathe in peace and calm; breathe out all your stress and anxiety. Let go of any problems or annoyances from your day. Visualize the light slowly permeating through you, filling your entire being with tranquility, leaving no room for tension or negativity.

Repeat this for at least ten minutes or until all the negativity has left your body. When you are finished, ground any excess energy by releasing it into the earth.

ENERGY EXERCISES

Another important part of ritual and magick is raising energy. This can be accomplished in a number of ways: meditation, chanting, singing, and dancing.

In this section you will learn a few simple exercises for raising and manipulating energy.

TREE ENERGY EXERCISE

Sit outside at the base of a tree. Close your eyes, ground and center yourself. Spend a few moments meditating, connecting with the energy of the tree nearby.

When you're ready, visualize yourself as the tree. Feel roots sprout from the base of your spine, burrowing into the cool earth below you. Feel them sink into the nutrient rich soil, soaking up the clean, refreshing water deep below.

Tilt your head back and stretch your arms above you, spreading your fingers out like branches. Feel the fiery sun warm your face, the breeze gently flowing along your arms and through your fingers. Feel your skin absorbing the life giving energy of sun and air. Feel the solid earth and refreshing water beneath you, giving you strength and vitality.

When you inhale, visualize your roots drawing the earth's energy up into your spine, your trunk. Feel it roll up your body, extending up into the branches of your arms, mixing with the sun's fiery energy and the cool breeze rustling through your leaves.

When you exhale, feel this energy disperse through your branches, releasing and changing into life-giving oxygen.

Allow your body to absorb the strength and vitality of the earth, the cool water, letting their essence mingle with the brisk air and the fiery sun. Feel the energies of the elements roll through you, strengthening and reviving you.

When you're ready, lower your arms, retracting your branches and slowly draw your roots up from the earth. Ground yourself by visualizing the earth beneath you absorbing any excess energy.

ENERGY BALL EXERCISE

This exercise teaches you to raise energy and direct it into your hands or other body parts, which is essential for certain types of spells and rituals.

Sit comfortably and center yourself, breathing slowly and deeply. When you're ready, begin rubbing your hands together briskly. Do you feel how warm they're becoming? That is the energy you're creating through friction.

When your hands are sufficiently warmed up, hold them a few inches apart from one another, palms facing each other. Focus on the heat you generated moments before, visualizing it as a bright ball of energy between your palms.

There is energy inside all of us that we can move and direct at our will. Focus your energy into the palms of your hands, feeling that heat and warmth as you hold this ball of energy.

Slowly, widen the space between your hands, pulling them further away from each other. Visualize the ball growing getting larger and brighter as you separate your hands, continuing to focus on the energy's warmth.

If you are no longer able to feel the tingle of the energy, rub your hands together for another moment and maintain that energy for as long as you can.

The more you practice this exercise, the easier it will become and you will find yourself able to maintain that energy ball in your hands for longer periods of time.

Once you are able to maintain this ball of energy for several minutes, try moving it to different parts of your body, feeling the corresponding tingle of warmth.

Note: This technique is fantastic for healing. For example, if you have a sore knee, stomach pains, or a headache, do this exercise and bring that ball of light to whatever area is bothering you. As you push that energy into the area, visualize this white light healing the injury or malady.

SENSING ENERGY AROUND YOU

Once you become adept at manipulating your own energy, you can begin to manipulate the energy in objects around you.

Every object has its own energy. Natural items like plants and stones have unique elemental energies that we can tap into in order to strengthen our own magick.

To attune yourself to this energy, choose a plant, herb or stone. Close your eyes and breathe deeply, bringing yourself into a meditative state.

Taking slow deep breaths, place your dominant hand over the item. Feel its inner energy in your hand. This might feel like a tingle, a dull throbbing, or warm hum in the palm of your hand. What emotions or sensations do you feel? Do any colors or images come to mind? Does it feel soothing? Energizing? Protective?

Open your senses and allow yourself to become receptive to whatever energies the plant or stone may hold.

Try this on different natural items, noticing the different sensations, colors, images, and emotions they evoke.

Once you've felt the energy of natural items, try this with other objects. Even man-made items contain energy; some of this will be from the natural materials that make it up, but they may also contain energy absorbed from their environment and the people who have used them or created them.

Old jewelry is a great object to practice this with, as it will have absorbed the energies of the people who have worn it in the past. Hold the item in your dominant hand and close your eyes, opening yourself up to any sensations, thoughts, or emotions.

Once you become adept at sensing this energy, you can begin directing your own energy into other items.

For example, after harvesting herbs or vegetable from your garden, it is a good idea to thank the earth for its sacrifice by sharing a portion of your energy with it. This can be done by holding your hand out to whatever plant you took from and sending a little of your energy out from your hand into the plant.

You can also create empowered charms and amulets by directing your energy into stones or jewelry to suit your own magickal needs.

CREATING CHARMS AND AMULETS

To create a magickal charm or amulet, you will first have to decide what kind of charm you wish to create.

Do you generally feel stressed at work and would like an amulet to keep you relaxed and calm? Do you have a big test coming up and need a charm to strengthen your mental acuity and help you retain information? Do you want to protect your home or yourself from danger or negativity? Do you need an energy boost for a project you're working on?

Once you have decided on a purpose for this charm, now you must choose what item you wish to imbue with power. I prefer jewelry that I can wear in everyday situations, but you can also choose stones or other small objects you can easily carry on you, or you might prefer something decorative you can hang in your home or near your front door for protection. Choose something suitable to the purpose of your charm.

Before beginning any magick, make sure you purify this object to cleanse it of any previous energy (You will find a cleansing ritual at the end of Chapter 3).

After you've purified the item, place it on your altar (if you have a pentacle, you can place it on that) and hold your hands over it.

Now focus on the purpose of this charm, whether it's for stress relief, inspiration, study help, protection, etc. Concentrate on your need, clearly visualizing exactly what you want this charm to do.

Meditate on this purpose, feeling the energy inside rise up to your call. You can even write up a short chant to repeat over and over to help focus your mind and raise energy. It can be something simple, like "Wealth, money, and prosperity to me," or something more flowery, such as "Lord and Lady, I beseech thee, peace and relaxation bestow upon me."

When you can feel the energy humming through your body, focus it into your hands and push it outward into the item you've chosen. Visualize the energy physically leaving your body and flowing into the item. You will know it has worked when you can feel the item pulsating with this energy.

When you've finished, ground yourself, releasing any excess energy into the earth.

Don't be surprised if you find yourself fatigued after this. Empowering objects requires a lot of energy. Make sure to eat something to replenish yourself.

CHAPTER 3: BASICS TOOLS

Tools are not strictly necessary—you can create powerful magick without them if you so choose. Consequently, you can go out and buy every item on this list, and if you don't have the focus and the willpower to create the change you seek, your magick will still fall flat.

Power comes from you, not the tools. However, tools can certainly help, and whether or not you choose to use them in your rituals, you should still be familiar with these basic items.

BOOK OF SHADOWS

A book of shadows is a Witch's personal record of spells, rituals, correspondences, mediations, and lessons. It is your go-to book when planning your next ritual or spell. Even if you choose not to use any other tool listed in this chapter, I highly recommend that you keep a book of shadows (BOS).

Some Witches prefer an elaborate leather bound tome as their book of shadows. Others like the ease of three-ring-binders or composition notebooks. Some even prefer to keep a digital book of shadows on their computer.

Personally, I like to use three-ring-binders with plastic sheet protectors for my BOS. I find it much easier to organize my book into different sections for correspondences, herbal work, invocations to the God and Goddess, sabbat rituals, stone work, divination, healing spells, protection rituals, etc.

Whatever you choose to use, make sure you record all spells and rituals you perform and their effects—whether they worked, how you felt during it, if you received any visions, messages, or psychic feelings. Make note of what worked and what you would change if you were to do it over.

You never know when you might want to repeat a particular spell or ritual and it is immeasurably helpful to have all of your rituals and notes organized in one place.

CANDLES

Candles are one of the most common items you will use in your spells and rituals. I recommend having a supply of many different colors to fit any spell you may need, however white can always be substituted if you do not have the specific color for a spell.

Candles come in many different sizes: large pillars, slim tapers, even tiny birthday candles can be used in your spellwork! These tiny candles are especially useful for when a spell requires the candle to burn down completely.

A candle snuffer is another item you might want to have handy. Some Witches discourage blowing out a candle used in spellwork, claiming that doing so blows away the magickal energy of the candle. Snuffing or pinching out the flame tend to be the recommended methods for putting out a spelled candle (though I can never pinch out a candle without burning myself!).

But if you don't own a candle snuffer and don't want to risk scorching your fingertips, then don't stress. I've never noticed a significant difference in my spells when blowing out a candle rather than snuffing it. Do whatever is most comfortable for you.

BESOM

One can't think the word "witch" without images of broomsticks coming to mind. It might surprise you to learn that Witches actually DO use brooms—just not for riding around on!

A Witch's broom, or besom, isn't used for flying but for sweeping away negative energy and creating sacred space.

You can use a regular household broom or the smaller, decorative brooms found at many arts and crafts stores. You can even use a branch from a tree or bush.

Feel free to decorate it to your own personal taste. You can wrap ribbons around the handle and attach natural or synthetic flowers and greenery to it if you want. Use your imagination! These tools are yours and should reflect your unique personality and energy.

CAULDRON

Like the broom, the cauldron is another item often associated with the word 'witch'. It's featured in nearly every book, play, or movie about witches.

The cauldron represents the Goddess's womb; it is the place of rebirth and creation. In times past, it was used for cooking and brewing potions and healing concoctions. These days, they can still be used for mixing potions, but are also used for burning incense, scrying (when filled with water), or burning items for a spell (such as a piece of paper, leaves, or herbs).

Cauldrons these days are usually relatively small, either ceramic or cast iron, but any steel or ceramic bowl could be used (just make sure the bowl is fireproof if you intend to burn anything in it).

WAND

A wand directs your energy outside your body, generally during circle casting. A wand can be easily made from a stick or tree branch. If you want, you can look up magickal properties of different types of wood and choose what resonates with you. Here are a few common types:

Apple: Love, healing, garden magick

Ash: Protection, prosperity, health

Birch: Protection, purification, banishing

Dogwood: Wishes, protection

Maple: Love, money, longevity

Oak: Protection, health, healing, fertility, money, luck

Pine: Healing, fertility, protection, banishing, money

Willow: Divination, love, protection, healing

Cut the branch to length (about 18 inches or as long as you're comfortable with). If you take the branch from a live tree, make sure to thank the tree for its sacrifice and allow the wood to dry for several days. Then, if you want to remove the bark, use a knife to carefully strip it away and smooth the surface.

You can also carve words, symbols, or runes into the wood or decorate it with paint, ribbon, or stones. Some witches prefer to keep the bark for a more natural feel. As always, do what feels best for you.

ATHAME

An athame is a dagger used in rituals for directing energy, much the same as a wand. Traditionally, it is a double edged blade with a black handle, though you can use whatever feels comfortable to you.

CENSER

A censer is another name for an incense burner. It is important to have a safe place to burn incense if you choose to do so in your rituals.

Personally, I love using incense in my spells and rituals; the scent really helps me to focus on raising energy and puts me in the right frame of mind for magick. You can find many elaborate censers online or you can use something as simple as a fireproof dish (seashells work well too!) with sand at the bottom to absorb the heat from the incense or charcoal.

BOLINE

A boline is a small knife, usually with a white handle. While the athame is only used for magickal workings, the boline is meant for more practical uses, such as engraving symbols on candles, cutting herbs, and carving wands.

PENTACLE

This is a wooden or ceramic disk with a pentacle drawn or engraved onto it. You can make this yourself by purchasing a flat wooden disk and painting or carving a five pointed star onto it.

The pentacle represents the element earth and can also be used for charging and empowering amulets and tools.

CLEANSING RITUAL FOR TOOLS

As you learned in Chapter 3, objects absorb the energies around them. This is why it's important to cleanse any ritualistic tools you plan on using: you don't know what energies may have been absorbed by previous owners and environments that may affect your spells.

Tools can be cleansed with salt, water, fire, incense, moonlight, sunlight, or by burying them in the earth. Be smart about it; certain items, like your athame or other metals, shouldn't be soaked in water for long periods of time or they'll rust. Stones and other items can be damaged by direct heat. Water may stain fabrics or ruin leather. Be practical in how you cleanse your items so you don't end up damaging them.

The following is a cleansing ritual I routinely use. It's simple, but effective.

What You Need:

White candle

Sage or Lavender Incense

A bowl of water

A small dish of salt

It isn't necessary to cast a circle for this ritual, but you can if you'd like. (See Chapter 4 for instructions on circle casting.)

Sit comfortably on the ground, with your items in front of you. Light the incense and candle, then close your eyes and breathe deeply.

Concentrate on your breath, slowly filling your lungs to their capacity then releasing it gently. Feel the energy of the earth beneath you rise up and enter your body. Imagine the water's energy in your own blood, beating through your veins. Feel the fire's energy from the candle, warming the air. Breathe in the energy from the incense smoke, wafting through the room.

When you can clearly feel the energies of the elements around you, find your center and open your eyes.

Pass the item or tool you wish to cleanse through the incense smoke while saying:

I cleanse this (___) in the name of Air. As I will, so mote it be.

Visualize the air's energy blowing all the negative energies away. Now face the candle and pass the item through the flame. (Be careful not to burn yourself or scorch the item!) Say:

I cleanse this (___) in the name of Fire. As I will, so mote it be.

Visualize the fire's energy burning all the negative energies away. Then dip your fingers into the water and sprinkle it over the item. Say:

I cleanse this (___) in the name of Water. As I will, so mote it be.

Visualize the water's energy washing away the negative energies. Sprinkle the salt over the item and say:

I cleanse this (___) in the name of Earth. As I will, so mote it be.

Visualize the earth's energy absorbing all the negative energies.

Now place both hands over the item and send your own energy out into it. Visualize the item filling with your own personal essence, chasing away any stray energy that may be left over. Say:

I cleanse this (__) in the name of Spirit. As I will, so mote it be.

Store your items in a safe place and repeat this ritual whenever you feel they need to be cleansed.

CHAPTER 4: SIMPLE CIRCLE CASTING

Casting a circle is a way to create sacred space, preparing the area for magick. It creates a barrier that holds in the energy raised during the ritual or spell, and blocks out any disruptive energies that may interfere with your magick.

While casting a circle isn't required for every spell or ritual, it should be done whenever you call upon spirits in case you inadvertently call any spirits or energies that may wish to linger. It's also useful to contain energy when you want to cast particularly powerful spells.

There are many different ways to cast a circle, ranging from the simplistic to the elaborate and complex. Since my purpose in this book is to teach easy, practical rituals and spells, I will outline a simple ritual for circle casting. If you find you want to elaborate upon this, by all means, feel free to add your own personal touches or chants.

Basic Steps

- Set up Altar and Prepare Circle
- Cast Circle
- Invoke the Elements
- Invoke the Deities
- Perform the Ritual or Spell
- Thanking the Deities
- Thanking and Releasing the Elements
- Open Circle

SET UP ALTAR AND PREPARE CIRCLE

Many Witches have a permanent altar in their home that holds their ritual tools and magickal items. You can decorate your altar any way you wish, with statues of the God and Goddess, candles, special crystals, plants, herbs, or flowering tree branches symbolizing the season.

If you don't have space for a large altar, or don't want to display your ritual tools so obviously, you could choose a simpler form, made from a small end table or shelf on the wall and decorate it with a few natural items representing the elements, such as a sea shell for water, a candle for fire, a bird feather or incense cone for air and a stone for earth.

Maintaining an altar is a great way to keep in touch with the spirit of the season. Each morning before starting your day you may want to stand or kneel before your altar and meditate for a few moments, communing with the God and Goddess or connecting to the earth's energy.

If you aren't able to maintain a permanent altar, then you can simply create a make-shift altar on any stable surface before each ritual and take it down afterwards. However, I would recommend creating a small area designated specifically for meditating and communing with the Deities. Having a special place that is only for prayer, meditation, and strengthening your bond with the Divinity will create positive energies in that area, making you more relaxed and helping you to slip into an altered state of consciousness more easily.

If you have a permanent altar, then make sure there is enough room around it to cast your circle.

Gather all of the items your ritual or spell requires and arrange them on your altar. Don't forget a lighter for your candles and incense!

If you want to, you can use a besom to sweep the area free of negative energy before setting up.

In each of the cardinal directions around the altar, place a candle to represent the elemental quarter. You can use all white candles if you want, or you can use the colors representative of each element (yellow for east/air; red for south/fire; blue for west/water; green for north/earth.)

Alternatively, if you can't or don't want to use candles, you can place other objects in the quarters to outline the circle. You could use stones, sea shells, plants, flowers, even a cord or ribbon. Do whatever feels right for you.

CAST CIRCLE

Once the altar and circle are physically set up, it's time to cast the circle. To do that, first center yourself and your energies. I like to sit in the center of the circle for a few minutes and meditate on the ritual I'm about to perform.

Once you've centered yourself, stand and call up energy from deep inside you. Feel it rise from your center, filling your chest, then push it outward into your projective, or dominant, hand while tracing the outline of the circle in a clockwise direction. If you choose to use a wand or athame, then you would hold that item in your projective hand and use it to direct the energy you send out. If not, then simply trace the circle using your index finger.

The important part here is focus and visualization. Feel the energy inside you bursting outward, forming a magickal barrier around the circle. Visualize it as a glowing wall of energy, encircling the entire space, extending above and below to encase you in a glowing sphere of pulsing energy. You need to be able to really feel this, to see it as if it is actually there. If you have difficulty with this, practice the visualization techniques listed in Chapter 2.

INVOKE THE ELEMENTS

When the circle is cast and you are surrounded by a sphere of magickal energy, it is time to invoke the elements and Deities.

Many Witches choose to create their own elemental invocations and chants. These can be as lengthy and elaborate as you want, or simply a line or two asking for their presence, such as *"Here in the East I call upon Air. Bless me with your presence here."*

Feel free to create your own quarter calls or use mine. Or, if you want, don't say anything at all. It is perfectly acceptable to call upon them in your mind. The words aren't important; your focus and will is. You have to open yourself up to the elements' energies and invite them into your circle. Whether you prefer to call upon them out loud or silently, it doesn't matter, as long as you are able to focus and feel their energy.

Start in the eastern quarter and say this or something similar:

Air of knowledge and creativity,
Please be present here with me.

Then close your eyes and open yourself up to air's energy. Focus on the scent of the incense, if you chose to use it, and feel air's energy hum through your body. Focus on your breath, on air's life-giving energy in your lungs. Feel its essence enter your circle, lending its strength and power to your ritual. Now face south and say:

Fire of health and vitality,
Please be present here with me.

Close your eyes and open yourself up to fire's energy. Focus on the heat coming from the candle flames, imagine fire's essence rising up and entering your body. Feel it along your skin, in the blood pumping through your veins. Imagine its vital energy filling your circle, lending its strength and power to your ritual.

Now face west and say:

Water of life and purity,
Please be present here with me.

Close your eyes and open yourself up to water's energy. Focus on its cool, soothing power. Hear the ocean waves gently lapping at the shore, feel a light rain soft upon your skin. Imagine water's soft energy entering your circle, lending its strength and power to your ritual.

Now face the north and say:

Earth of strength and security,
Please be present here with me.

Close your eyes and open yourself up to earth's energy. Focus on the earth's steady presence. Feel the roughness of tree bark beneath your hands, the solid and dependable energy of the earth below your feet. Visualize its green energy seeping up from the ground, drawn up into your feet, moving up your legs, into your torso and chest. Feel it expand, filling your body and outward, entering your circle, lending its strength and power to your ritual.

INVOKE THE DEITIES

Once the elements are invoked, stand in the center and call upon the God and Goddess, inviting Them into your circle. What you say is up to you. You can find some very beautiful invocations online, or you can say a silent, heartfelt prayer to Them that comes to you while you're in the moment. I've included my personal invocations below. Feel free to use them if you want or alter them to suit your needs.

Since Wicca is about our personal relationship to the Deities, you should use this time to strengthen your bond and commitment to Them. Allow your heart and energy to open to Them and you will feel Their presence around you.

INVOCATION TO THE GODDESS

Goddess of the Earth and Sea,
Who showers love and light on me.
You illuminate the moon and set the tide,
You are my beacon, my teacher, my guide.

I call on you this sacred night,

To bless me and this magickal rite.

Fill me with your presence true,

My mind, my heart, my soul, to you. (Gently touch your head, heart, and

lips, then raise your hand up in offering to the Goddess.)

Pause for a few moments, feeling the Goddess's presence fill you and surround you.

INVOCATION TO THE GOD

God of the wild forest and field,

You are my guardian and my shield.

You are the sun's radiant fire,

Your light shines down to illuminate and inspire.

I call on you this sacred night,

To bless me in this magickal rite.

Fill me with your presence true,

My mind, my heart, my soul, to you. (Gently touch your head, heart, and

lips, then raise your hand up in offering to the God.)

Pause for a few moments, feeling the God's presence fill you and surround you.

PERFORM THE RITUAL OR SPELL

This is the bulk of your ritual. This is where you'd celebrate the sabbat, hold your ritual, or cast a spell; whatever your intended purpose for casting this circle was. When you're finished, ground and center yourself.

THANKING THE DEITIES

Once your ritual is complete it is time to thank the God and Goddess for Their presence. You can simply say a silent prayer of thanks or you can recite a more ritualized farewell. As always, do what feels comfortable.

PRAYER OF THANKS

Lord and Lady, I thank you for your presence tonight.
May you always keep me in your love and light.

THANKING AND RELEASING THE ELEMENTS

Now it is time to thank and release the elements you invoked earlier. Start in the east and work deosil (clockwise) around the circle. As you release each element, visualize its energy leaving, dissipating from the circle.

East

Air of knowledge and creativity,
Many thanks and blessed be.

South

Fire of health and vitality,
Many thanks and blessed be.

West

Water of life and purity,
Many thanks and blessed be.

North

Earth of strength and security,
Many thanks and blessed be.

OPEN CIRCLE

After releasing the elements, you need to open the circle. To do this, start in the east and point your wand (or athame or your hand) at the circle's boundary on the ground. Moving clockwise, visualize the energy being sucked back up. See the energy returning from where it came, feel it tingling in your hand. Say this or something similar:

The circle is open, but never broken. Merry meet, merry part, and merry meet again!

CHAPTER 5: SABBAT RITUALS AND SPELLS

Wiccans celebrate eight seasonal festivals based upon the solar calendar and ancient Pagan practices. This chapter will give you a brief introduction and overview for each sabbat along the wheel of the year, as well as suggestions for rituals, spells, or celebrations for each.

YULE

Yule, also known as the Winter Solstice, is the shortest day of the year. The exact date varies from year to year based upon the solar calendar but generally falls on or around December 21st.

Night reigns the longest on the Winter Solstice, and every day after it, daylight lasts a little longer. Consequently, this day has become associated with the rebirth of God and the sun.

After His symbolic death at Samhain, the God is reborn anew from the Goddess, just as the sun is reborn and the days begin lengthening. Fires and candles are lit in honor of the God's birth and the return of the sun. It is a reminder to us that in death, there is rebirth, and all of life is cyclical.

It also teaches us that hope can be found even in our darkest hours. Things may look bleak, the landscape may be frozen and barren, but the sun has returned and every day after this, things will get a little bit brighter.

The same concept can be applied to our own lives; no matter how bad things may get, there is always hope for a better year ahead, a brighter future. Spring will return and bring with it warmth and renewal.

Although the Celtic Wiccan tradition celebrates Samhain as the New Year, much of the modern world holds December as the end of the calendar year. With the rebirth of the sun comes a new year, one which we hope will be prosperous and joyful.

YULE ACTIVITY FOR A PROSPEROUS NEW YEAR

In keeping with this theme of rebirth, renewal, and hope for a brighter future, one fun activity around this time is creating your own Yule tree decorations to help bring about a prosperous new year!

First, decide what it is you hope to bring about this coming year. Do you long for love? A promotion or new job? Wisdom and knowledge? Luck or wealth?

Whatever your hopes are for the coming year, you need to decide on an ornament or symbol to represent it. A heart could represent love, a coin for money or wealth, a clover for luck, a book for knowledge, etc. Choose whatever symbol you feel best represents what you hope to find this next year.

Once you've decided on your symbol or symbols, it's time to create an ornament from it. This can be done in a number of ways: One way would be to repurpose old items.

If it's love you seek, look through your old jewelry for a heart shaped locket or charm. For a prosperity ornament, maybe you want to hunt through your old coin collection to find a silver dollar to use rather than an ordinary nickel or quarter.

If you can't find anything around the house to suit your needs, you could purchase something to represent your wish for the New Year or you could create your own ornaments using wooden discs from a hardware store or hobby shop. You can paint or carve symbols, words, and pictures into these. Alternatively, many shops around this time of year sell clear baubles to paint your own ornaments. You could even fashion your own out of clay if you want.

Whatever you choose—to use something you already own, purchase something new, or create your own unique ornaments—you're going to need to cleanse these items before charming them (see Chapter 3 for cleansing instructions). Then you should charge them based on their purpose.

To do this, simply hold each one individually in your hands or over your pentacle (if you have one) and focus on the charm's intention—prosperity, fertility, love, good fortune— whatever it is that you wish to bring about in the next year, visualize it coming to pass. Picture it in your mind as if it is happening at this moment.

Inhale, feeling your energy respond, rising up and answering your call. When you exhale, push this energy out through your hands, into the ornament. Feel the charm warm beneath your hands; visualize it glowing with power and purpose.

Do this for each ornament you created. Once finished, hang them on your Yule tree in order to bring your hopes and wishes for the New Year to fruition!

IMBOLC

Imbolc, also known as Brigid's Day, is observed on February 2nd, halfway between the Winter Solstice and the Spring Equinox. Imbolc was originally a festival celebrating the onset of ewe's lactation and the birthing of lambs. Ewe's milk was an important source of sustenance to our ancestors, and thus made this a time of great joy. It was a sign that winter's hardships were ending and spring was on its way with all her bounties.

This festival was also a celebration of Brigid, the beloved Goddess of poetry, healing, and smithcraft. Her many gifts are all associated with fire: the light of wisdom and inspiration, the warmth of hearth and home, and the fires of the forge and metalcrafting. In Her Maiden aspect this time of year, she brings life and fertility to the land.

Traditionally, Imbolc is also a time to cleanse the home and hearth, sweeping away the old energies of the waning winter to make way for the fresh, clean energies of the coming spring. The following ritual is a great way to cleanse your home of any stale, disruptive energy.

HOUSE CLEANSING CANDLE SPELL

This is best if done at sunset on Imbolc, but it can be used any time you feel the energies in your home need to be cleansed and refreshed.

What You Need:

White candle

Candle holder that is safe to walk around with

     As you light the candle, say a quick prayer of honor and welcome to Brigid, the Fire Maiden:

> _Beloved Brigid, Lady of fire and the hearth._
> _Goddess of light and inspiration, Protectress of new births._
> _I welcome you into my home and ask for your blessing bright._
> _Cleanse this space of negativity; purify it with your light!_

     Now, with candle in hand, start in one room of your house and slowly walk clockwise around it, allowing the light from the flame to shine in every corner, nook and cranny. Visualize the firelight cleansing the room and chasing away the stale or negative energy.

     When you've circled the space, allowing the light to shine on all areas of the room, stand in the center and close your eyes. Visualize the light cast from the candle growing bigger and brighter, swirling clockwise around the room, heating it, purifying everything it touches. You'll know it's working when you feel a shift in the energy around you. The air in the room will feel lighter and cleaner.

     If you don't feel a shift in the energy, or you sense any lingering negativity, circle the room again, making sure to concentrate on purifying the entire room. Open up closets to allow the candlelight to shine into these often overlooked areas (be careful not to get the candle too close to anything flammable!)

When you've finished cleansing the room, move onto the next, making your way throughout the house, cleansing each room one by one. Don't forget bathrooms, hallways, and stairwells. All areas of the house should be cleansed—no room is too small or unimportant.

When you've cleansed every room, say a short prayer of thanks to Brigid for blessing your home:

Blessed Brigid, Lady of home and hearth,
Thank you for your light and warmth.
Bless this space with love, pure and bright,
Lady of the Flame, thank you for your presence tonight.

OSTARA

Ostara, also known as the Vernal or Spring Equinox, falls on or around March 21st. This is the official first day of spring. On Ostara, the hours of day and night are equal in length. After today, daylight hours will start to overtake night.

This is a time of adolescence for the Maiden Goddess and Youthful God and a joyous celebration of new life after the desolation of winter.

Eggs and rabbits figure prominently this time of year, symbolizing fertility and rebirth, as do spring flowers like crocuses, tulips, daffodils, and hyacinth.

PLANTING AN HERB GARDEN

Ostara is a great time to take advantage of the spring's fertile energy by planting an herb garden. Herbs are an integral part of many spells and rituals. They can be burned on charcoal as incense, added to sachets to attract love or wealth, sprinkled around your house for protection, placed under your pillow for peaceful sleep or prophetic dreams, brewed in healing teas and potions, etc. Choose the herbs that speak to you, and those that you are most likely to use in your spells and rituals.

Below is a list of some common herbs and their magickal uses. These should be relatively easy to find and will make a great addition to any magickal garden.

LIST OF COMMON HERBS

Basil: Love, Protection, Wealth, Banishing Negativity

Catmint: Love, Beauty, Joy, Feline Magick

Dill: Protection, Wealth, Luck, Love, Sexuality

Lavender: Love, Happiness, Protection, Purification, Peace, Sleep

Lemon Balm: Love, Lust, Purification, Happiness, Success,

Mint: Wealth, Healing, Protection, Purification, Banishing Negativity, Lust, Energy, Vitality,

Mugwort: Lust, Fertility, Strength, Healing, Protection, Psychic Abilities and Dreams

Parsley: Protection, Purification, Lust, Fertility

Rosemary: Protection, Healing, Purification, Love, Lust, Beauty, Banishing Negativity, Peaceful Sleep, Aids Mental Retention and Knowledge

Sage: Purification, Protection, Aids Mental Retention, Wisdom, Wish Magick

Thyme: Loyalty, Love, Strength, Courage, Purification, Healing, Sleep, Psychic Powers,

*For a more complete list of herbs and their magickal properties, see Chapter 6.

You can find most of these herbs at your local garden center, either as plants or seeds. When you've prepared the garden bed and planted the seeds or plants, sit near your new garden. Spend some time meditating on the budding season, opening yourself up to its energies.

Say the following dedication while visualizing positive energy flowing from you into the earth.

GARDEN DEDICATION

Youthful Lord and Virgin Maid,
I ask for your blessing and your aid.
In celebration of Ostara and the spring's rebirth,
I enrich this soil and awaken the earth.
In your honor I plant these seeds,
Bless this garden, protecting it from weeds.
Shine your light upon this plot of earth,
Bringing strength, fertility, joy, and mirth.
Blessed Be!

BELTANE

Beltane, also called May Day, is celebrated on April 30th or May 1st. It is a joyous celebration of the sacred marriage between the God and Goddess. On Beltane, the God impregnates the Goddess, bringing fertility to the earth.

Maypoles are commonly used during May Day festivities. The wooden pole is a phallic symbol representing the God, while the colored ribbons woven around it represent the Goddess sheathing the God, bringing fertility to the earth.

Beltane is also a celebration of the strengthening sun, and is as much a fire festival as it is a fertility festival. Bonfires are commonly held to welcome the upcoming summer. It's believed that the smoke from these bonfires will purify people, pets, and livestock and bring blessings of prosperity and good fortune.

This is a day of joy, celebration, and frivolity. It is a great time to throw a party to rejoice in the coming summer. So, live it up, enjoy the day! Invite friends and family over, light a bonfire, and feast on cakes and sweets. Revel in the continuity of the fertile earth and the long summer days of light and warmth ahead!

MINI MAYPOLE SUCCESS SPELL

If you ever have the opportunity to participate in a maypole dance, I strongly recommend you take it! Dancing around the maypole is tremendous fun and a fantastic way to welcome in the spring.

However, even if you aren't able to erect a 20-foot pole in your yard, or you don't know enough Wiccans or Pagans to have a maypole dance, that doesn't mean you can't partake of this time honored tradition on a smaller scale.

This time of year is full of potential and fertility and you can use this energy to grow in your own life, in your career, in your spirituality. The following Maypole activity will help you to harness the magick of the season and allow this fertility to manifest in your life, helping you to achieve your hopes and goals.

What You Need:

A straight branch or wooden dowel about 18 inches long

Marker

Four pieces of colored ribbon about 3 feet long each. Spring colors like lavender, yellow, light blue and green work well, or you can coordinate the colors to the wishes they represent: gold for prosperity, green for fertility, red for love, etc. (See Chapter 6 for the full list of color correspondences.)

On each ribbon, use the marker to write a wish or goal you have for the coming months, then tie the ribbons to the top of your pole.

Spend a few moments meditating upon the new season's energies. Feel the dormant energy of summer, just waiting to burst forth into life. Feel the hum of new growth just below the earth's surface. Harness this energy, absorbing it into yourself, and focus it towards your goals.

Now braid the ribbons around the pole while visualizing your wishes and goals manifesting in your life.

When you're finished, you can display your maypole on your altar or outside in your garden, keeping it safe until

Samhain, when you can detach the ribbons and burn them, scattering their ashes into your garden.

LITHA

Also known as Midsummer or the Summer Solstice, Litha occurs on or around June 21st and marks the longest day of the year. The sun is at its zenith, the God at the peak of His power. Today marks the beginning of summer, and we celebrate this new season of warmth, growth, and fertility.

According to Litha lore, Midsummer is also the time of the battle between the Oak King and the Holly King. The Oak King has ruled since Yule as the sun slowly strengthened. But today marks a turning point. Tonight, the Holly king is crowned as he defeats the Oak King in battle. He will rule under the waning sun until Yule, when they do battle once more.

Like Beltane, this is also a fire festival and bonfires are a traditional part of the celebration. Midsummer is also a great day to harvest magickal and medicinal herbs. It's said that any herbs harvested on this day are more potent than those collected on any other day of the year.

With the earth full of life and the sun at its peak, Litha is one of the most magickal days of the year. The very air vibrates with the energy of life, joy, and love. As such, Litha is the sabbat most closely associated with fairy lore.

It's believed that on the Summer Solstice the Fey are out in vast numbers, dancing in fields and forests to celebrate the beginning of summer. It's tradition to leave a gift of honeyed bread or cakes for the Fey and other nature spirits to honor them and ask for their blessings on your home and gardens.

MIDSUMMER LOVE SPELL

Midsummer is a great day for all magick, particularly love spells. Before beginning any love spell, it is imperative you understand that you should never cast this spell on a specific person. If you cast a charm to make a specific person fall in love with you, you are taking away their free will. Remember the law "an you harm none, do what ye will"? Forcing a person to fall in love with you constitutes harm, and you will find that your spell goes awry.

Rather than trying to force someone into loving you, you should instead ask for love to be brought into your life. Ask the God and Goddess to send you the lover or partner that is right for you, rather than trying to bend someone's will to your own.

What You Need:

Red or Pink candle

Red apple

Herbs (Optional): Lavender, Catmint, or Rose Petals

Light the candle and close your eyes, meditating upon the type of lover you wish to draw. Feel the energy of this magickal day flow through you, opening your heart to accept love and happiness. Visualize yourself finding your soul mate, your perfect partner. Know that you are worthy of love and devotion, and that the right person will come into your life in the near future.

When you are ready, hold the apple in your hands and repeat the following:

As Sun's fire burns bright in the sky high above,
I rejoice in earth's abundance, fertility, and love.
On Midsummer's day, fields fill with Fey and Fairy,
Celebrating the Summer Solstice, they dance and make merry.
As the earth rejoices in new growth and vitality,
I seek summer's warmth and sensuality.
True love do I call, a partner faithful and strong,
Bringing fulfillment and joy for many years to come.
Love and commitment invoked by Midsummer's Sun,
For the joy of us both, and may this harm none.

While visualizing yourself with your future partner, focus your energy, your need, your desire into the fruit.

Once the apple has absorbed the energy, bite into it, focusing on the tangy sweetness, the life giving sustenance, the vital energy you are consuming. Continue to visualize yourself finding your future lover as you eat the rest of the apple.

When only the core remains, go outside and bury it in the earth, sprinkling Lavender, Catmint, or Rose petals over it. Know that love will enter your life in the near future.

LUGHNASADH

Lughnasadh (pronounced LOO-nah-sah or loo-NAH-sah) takes place on August 1st and is the first of three harvest festivals. At this time, the first of the spring crops are ready for harvest and we give thanks to the God and Goddess for Their blessing and bounty.

The God's power is waning as the sun rides lower in the sky each day, the night slowly gaining strength. We grieve for His impending death and honor His sacrifice, evident in the harvested wheat, which dies in order to give us life and sustenance.

The Goddess is heavily pregnant at this time, just as the fields are heavy with ripening crops. Though She's saddened by the fading God, She nourishes His seed in Her womb and looks forward to His rebirth at Yule.

Lughnasadh is a time for contemplating the mysteries of life, death, and rebirth, and for giving thanks for all we have been blessed with in our lives.

CORN DOLLY PROSPERITY SPELL

As a harvest festival, Lughnasadh is also a time for reaping rewards from earlier efforts, just as we reap the bounty of seeds planted earlier in the year. The following is a spell to bring you prosperity, luck, and abundance in the months to come.

What You Need:

Corn husks

Yarn or string to tie the husks

Traditionally at this time, corn husks or wheat sheaves are fashioned into a dolly to represent the Grain or Harvest Mother. To create this corn dolly, you will need about five corn husks. Many stores sell dried corn husks for decorations at this time of year or you may choose to dry your own husks for this project.

Once you have your husks, trim the bottom and top part so they will lie flat, then soak them in water for 20 minutes to make them pliable.

Lay two husks on the table, one on top of the other, and place a few pieces of yarn along the center for the dolly's hair, allowing them to extend over the bottom edge of the husks by about an inch.

Now lay two more husks on top of the yarn, lining the narrow sides of the husks together. At the bottom of the husks where the yarn hangs over, tie the bundle tightly with string or yarn.

Holding the knot in your hand yarn side down, peel the first two layers of husk down over the knot, exposing the yarn hair inside. Do the same for the other side, so you have the corn husks pointing downward with the yarn at the top.

Create the head of the doll by tying a string around the husk, just below the knot inside.

To create the arms, tightly roll a single husk length-wise and insert it between the husks that make up the skirt, just under the head. Tie another string below the arms to keep them in place. If you wish, you can also tie a piece of yarn at the ends of the arms to create hands.

And now your corn dolly is complete! You can decorate it or paint words or symbols onto it if you wish.

Once your Grain Mother is created, it's time to bless her. Lay her on your altar or somewhere outside where she can feel the sun's rays.

Holding your hands over her, channel the abundant energy of the season into her and say:

Mother of the Harvest Grain, Goddess of Rebirth,
Your bounty feeds and nourishes everyone on Earth.
Father of the Midsummer Sun, God of Prosperity,
Your sunlight blesses all that it touches with life and fertility.
This corn dolly has basked in your bright sunny fields,
Filling her with the bounty of your abundant yields.
May her blessings of wealth and prosperity
Fill my home with good fortune and abundance plenty!

Now place the corn dolly in a safe place in your home. You may wish to display her on your altar until the end of the harvest season before storing her away for the winter. Her presence in your home will bring blessings of prosperity, wealth, and abundance to you and your family.

At Imbolc, she can be burned and her ashes scattered in your garden to encourage spring growth and fertility.

MABON

Mabon, also known as the Autumn Equinox, falls on or around September 21st. On the Autumn Equinox, day and night are equal in length. After this day, the sun begins to wane and the earth readies itself for the coming winter, just as the God prepares for His impending death at Samhain.

Mabon is the second harvest festival and the official start of fall. Sometimes known as the Witches' Thanksgiving, it is a time to give thanks to the God and Goddess for all we have been blessed with and to celebrate the bounty of the earth.

MABON THANKSGIVING RITUAL

As Mabon is a time to give thanks for all the blessings we have received, the following is a simple thanksgiving ritual, similar to the Tree Energy Exercise detailed in Chapter 2.

What You Need:

Offering plate or bowl

Food to be offered in thanks, such as apples, grapes, corn, grain, acorns, pine nuts, or even bird seed

Find a comfortable place outside where you won't be disturbed. Sit cross-legged on the earth and find your center.

Breathing deeply, open your senses to the energies around you. Feel the sun warming your skin, the breeze whispering through your hair, the earth, calm and steady, cradling your body.

Concentrate on the area at the base of your spine, the part of your body touching the earth beneath you. Visualize roots sprouting from here, burrowing into the soil, sinking deep into the earth below.

When you inhale, imagine those roots drawing energy up into your body from deep within the earth. Allow it to travel up along your spine, feeling its warmth tingle along your nerves. When you exhale, circle this energy throughout your whole body, allowing it to fill your chest, your abdomen, your mind.

With each breath, inhale the autumn's energies, feeling it swirl within you, filling you with the season's strength and spirit.

When you've absorbed all the energy you can, open your eyes and lift the offering you've prepared. Say the following while sending the energy from your hands into the offering:

After today, the night grows darker,
And the earth prepares for her winter slumber.
The long days of summer come to an end
As autumn sweeps in, stripping leaves from trees
And earth's bounty is harvested from Her fields.

I give thanks to the Lord of the Sun,

For His days of summer warmth and fun.

I give thanks to the Lady of the Field,

For Her life-giving and bountiful yield.

I thank you, Lord and Lady, for all that I have.

For all that I am.

For all that I will become.

Blessed be.

Take your offering and place it outside somewhere—at the base of a tree, the middle of a field, in a special place in your garden—anywhere wild animals will find it and be able to feast upon your gift.

SAMHAIN

October 31st, also known as Halloween, marks the Witches New Year in Celtic traditions. Samhain (pronounced SOW-en) is the third and final harvest festival. It is the day we say farewell to the God, who dies this night to be reborn at Yule.

This is the time when the veil between the physical and spiritual world is thinnest. During this time of year, we remember those who have passed before us. Many Witches use this time to commune with the spirits of their loved ones. It is also a time for us to reflect on the year that has passed and to contemplate the changes we wish to make in the future.

SAMHAIN RITUAL FOR BANISHING BAD HABITS

As Samhain marks the New Year in Celtic traditions, it is also a great time to focus on improving ourselves in the coming year. The following is a great spell to help you break any bad habits that have been holding you back.

What You Need:

Paper

Black candle

Fire proof dish or plate

Oil: Dragon's Blood (Optional)

Herb: Rosemary (Optional)

Think about the year that has passed. What have you accomplished? Is there anything you set out to do but never achieved? Is there anything holding you back from accomplishing these things in the coming year?

Perhaps you are holding onto anger or hurt over an old grudge. Maybe you just can't seem to find the energy to accomplish the goals you set for yourself, or you find yourself spending too much time on social media or watching TV. Are you overly negative about yourself, or do you procrastinate when you have a deadline to meet? Do you lack the motivation or energy to exercise as much as you'd like? What negative traits or bad habits would you get rid of if you could?

On a slip of paper, write down one or more traits or bad habits that you wish to banish, whether it be laziness, shyness, social media addiction, unhealthy eating habits, anger, procrastination, low self-esteem, depression, negativity, etc.

If you choose to use Dragon's Blood oil and Rosemary, anoint your candle with the oil, starting in the center of the candle and rubbing it outward to the ends. Then sprinkle the Rosemary onto a plate or dish and roll the candle in it so the herb sticks to the candle.

Place the candle in a sturdy holder and light it, then ground and center yourself.

Staring into the candle flame, think about the trait or habit you've chosen to banish. How has this held you back? How will you be better as a person with this gone?

Say this or something similar:

Lord and Lady of the night,
I call to you by candlelight.
As the Wheel keeps spinning round,
To these habits have I been bound.
Now, as the Wheel begins anew,
I banish (habit or trait) from all that I do.
Too long has it kept me chained,
Tonight, I break free from its restraint.

Now take your slip of paper and carefully light it with the flame from the candle and set it on a fireproof plate or dish to burn completely.

As the paper burns, visualize yourself free from the habit or habits that have been holding you back and say:

Candle black as midnight hour,

Purge this habit with your power.

I banish (habit or trait) and set myself free,

As I will so mote it be!

If possible, allow the candle to burn out completely and bury the remains of the candle and the ashes from the paper outside.

CHAPTER 6: CORRESPONDENCES FOR RITUAL DESIGN

This chapter will help you in creating your own spells for any need. When creating your own spell, you can incorporate colored candles, incense, oils, herbs, and stones into your rituals.

Adding correspondences into your spells is a great way to increase the effectiveness of your magick. As discussed in Chapter 2, all items contain their own unique energy. By adding items like herbs, stones, or colored candles into your spells and rituals, you can harness this energy for your own purposes.

COLORS

Color magick is one of the easiest ways to add correspondences into your spells and rituals. It can be used to coordinate different colored candles, clothing, ribbons, paint, etc.

Black: This color is generally used to repel or banish negative energies and for ridding yourself of bad habits. It represents the Crone aspect of the Goddess and can also be used for grounding, meditation, protection, defense, transformation, wisdom, and to stop gossip and lies.

Blue: Blue is calming, used for creating peace, tranquility, clarity, stress relief, protection, and healing. It can also be used for communication and bringing about psychic awareness. It is the color of the element water.

Brown: Brown is used in magick involving animals, such as healing or protecting pets. It is also the color of earth, and as such, it aids in grounding, stability, security, centering, common sense and decision making. It can also be used to find lost objects.

Green: Green is the color of Mother Earth, growth, abundance, fertility, healing, rejuvenation, and new beginnings. It is also used for prosperity, financial success, employment, and money.

Purple: Purple is the color of the fifth element, spirit, and as such is used in workings involving spiritual awakening, divination, psychic abilities, clairvoyance, and intuition. It is also the color of the Divinity and can be used to call for Their protection or to commune with the God and Goddess.

Lavender: Lavender is soothing and can be used to lift the mood, repel depression, calm tensions, relieve stress and anxiety, and bring out inner beauty.

Orange: Orange is used to stimulate energy, creativity, joy, motivation, and fun. It is also used for success, achieving business goals, and victory in legal matters.

Pink: Pink stimulates love of all kinds, whether romantic or friendship. It's used in magick involving love, friendship, harmony, romance, forgiveness, and compassion.

Red: Red is the color of passion, lust, fertility, power, strength, courage, vitality, health, and energy. It is also the color of the Triple Goddess in Her Mother aspect.

White: White is an all-purpose color, as it reflects all other colors. If you don't have a particular color candle you need, you can almost always substitute it for a white candle. White is also used in magick involving purity, cleansing, healing, peace, purification, innocence and protection. White is the color of the Triple Goddess in Her Maiden aspect.

Yellow: Yellow represents the element air and is used for all magick involving knowledge, intellect, memory, success, creativity, inspiration, joy, and cheerfulness.

Gold: Gold represents the God, and is used for magick involving fortune, wealth, success, prosperity, victory, and justice.

Silver: Silver is the Goddess's color and is used in magick involving the moon, dreams, and psychic abilities.

HERBS

Herbs are a common part of spells and rituals and can be used either in their original plant form, as dried herbs, oils, or incense.

Beauty: Avocado, Catmint, Flax, Ginseng, Rose, Rosemary

Courage: Cedar, Columbine, Sweet Pea, Thyme, Yarrow

Divination: Dandelion, Ground Ivy, Hazelnut, Hibiscus, Mugwort, Pomegranate

Fertility: Cucumber, Daffodil, Grape, Hazel, Mugwort, Nuts, Oak, Parsley, Pine, Pomegranate, Sunflower, Wheat

Friendship: Lemon, Passion Flower, Sunflower, Sweet Pea, Vanilla

Gossip (to stop): Clove, Rue, Slippery Elm, Snapdragon

Happiness: Catmint, Daisy, Honeysuckle, Hyacinth, Lavender, Lemon Balm, Marjoram, Morning Glory, Saffron

Health and Healing: Allspice, Apple, Cedar, Cinnamon, Cucumber, Ivy, Lemon Balm, Mint, Mugwort, Nutmeg, Pine, Rose, Rosemary, Sandalwood, Thyme, Vervain, Willow

Legal Matters: Buckthorn, Hickory, Marigold

Love: Apple, Apricot, Avocado, Basil, Bleeding Heart, Catmint, Chamomile, Cherry, Cinnamon, Clove, Columbine, Crocus, Daffodil, Daisy, Dill, Dragon's Blood, Fig, Hibiscus, Hyacinth, Jasmine,

Lavender, Lemon Balm, Maple, Marjoram, Peach, Poppy, Rose, Rosemary, Rue, Saffron, Strawberry, Thyme, Tulip, Vanilla, Vervain, Willow, Yarrow

Luck: Allspice, Anise, Daffodil, Hazel, Heather, Holly, Nutmeg, Oak, Orange, Poppy, Rose, Violet

Lust: Caraway, Carrot, Cinnamon, Dill, Hibiscus, Lemongrass, Lemon Balm, Mint, Mugwort, Parsley, Rosemary, Saffron, Vanilla, Violet

Mental Retention/Studying: Celery, Celery Seed, Forget-Me-Not, Lily of the Valley, Pansy, Periwinkle, Rosemary, Sage, Spearmint

Peace/Reduce Stress: Chamomile, Lavender, Morning Glory, Passion Flower, Vervain, Violet

Prophetic Dreams: Anise, Jasmine, Marigold, Mimosa, Mugwort, Rose

Prosperity: Alfalfa, Allspice, Almond, Basil, Bergamot, Chamomile, Cinnamon, Clover, Dill, Marjoram, Mint, Mugwort, Nutmeg, Oak, Orange, Pecan, Pine, Sunflower, Tulip, Vervain, Wheat

Protection: Aloe, Anise, Basil, Bay Leaf, Birch, Blackberry, Cactus, Carnation, Cedar, Cinnamon, Clove, Clover, Dill, Dogwood, Dragon's Blood, Eucalyptus, Foxglove, Frankincense, Holly, Ivy, Juniper, Lavender, Marigold, Mimosa, Mint, Mugwort, Oak, Parsley, Pine, Raspberry, Rose, Rosemary, Sage, Sandalwood, Snapdragon, Tulip, Vervain, Violet, Willow, Wintergreen, Witch Hazel

Psychic Abilities: Celery, Cinnamon, Honeysuckle, Lemongrass, Marigold, Mugwort, Peppermint, Rose, Rowan, Star Anise, Thyme, Yarrow

Purification: Anise, Basil, Bay Leaf, Cedar, Chamomile, Coconut, Lavender, Lemon, Lemon Balm, Mimosa, Mint, Parsley, Peppermint, Rosemary, Sage, Sandalwood, Thyme, Vervain

Sleep: Chamomile, Hops, Lavender, Peppermint, Rosemary, Thyme, Vervain

Success: Cinnamon, Clover, Ginger, Lemon Balm, Orange, Rowan

Wishes: Dandelion, Dogwood, Hazel, Sage, Sandalwood, Sunflower, Violet, Walnut

STONES

Stones can be carried as talismans, worn in jewelry, added to magickal sachets, or placed on your altar during spellwork to give your magick an added boost.

Amplification: Opal, Crystal Quartz

Beauty: Amber, Jasper, Opal, Rose Quartz,

Breaking Bad Habits: Moonstone, Obsidian, Onyx

Childbirth: Geode, Moonstone

Courage: Amethyst, Aquamarine, Bloodstone, Carnelian, Diamond, Lapis Lazuli, Tiger's-Eye, Turquoise

Dieting: Moonstone, Topaz

Divination: Amethyst, Azurite, Hematite, Moonstone, Obsidian, Opal, Tiger's-Eye, Crystal Quartz

Fertility: Green Agate, Garnet, Geode, Jade, Moonstone, Pearl

Friendship: Rose Quartz, Pink Tourmaline, Turquoise

Grounding: Black Tourmaline, Hematite, Moonstone, Obsidian, Salt

Happiness: Blue Agate, Amethyst, Lapis Lazuli, Orange Calcite, Smoky Quartz, Sunstone

Health and Healing: Green Agate, Amethyst, Aventurine, Bloodstone, Carnelian, Diamond, Garnet, Hematite, Jade, Lapis Lazuli, Peridot, Crystal Quartz, Smoky Quartz, Sapphire, Sunstone, Topaz, Turquoise

Love: Amber, Amethyst, Emerald, Jade, Lapis Lazuli, Moonstone, Pearl, Rose Quartz, Sapphire, Topaz, Pink Tourmaline, Turquoise

Luck: Amber, Aventurine, Opal, Pearl, Tiger's-Eye, Turquoise

Lust: Carnelian, Coral, Sunstone

Mental Retention/Studying: Aventurine, Citrine, Emerald, Fluorite, Crystal Quartz

Peace/Reduce Stress: Blue Agate, Amethyst, Aquamarine, Aventurine, Carnelian, Coral, Diamond, Obsidian, Sapphire, Sodalite, Blue Tourmaline

Physical Energy: Banded Agate, Moss Agate, Garnet, Crystal Quartz, Sunstone, Tiger's-Eye, Red Tourmaline

Prophetic Dreams: Amethyst, Azurite, Moonstone

Prosperity: Green Agate, Aventurine, Bloodstone, Emerald, Jade, Opal, Pearl, Peridot, Ruby, Sapphire, Tiger's-Eye, Topaz, Green Tourmaline

Protection: Agate, Amber, Carnelian, Citrine, Coral, Diamond, Emerald, Garnet, Jade, Lapis Lazuli, Moonstone, Obsidian, Onyx, Pearl, Peridot, Crystal Quartz, Ruby, Salt, Sunstone, Tiger's-Eye, Topaz, Black Tourmaline, Red Tourmaline

Psychic Abilities: Amethyst, Aquamarine, Azurite, Citrine, Emerald, Lapis Lazuli, Crystal Quartz

Purification: Aquamarine, Salt

Sleep: Amethyst, Moonstone, Peridot, Blue Tourmaline

MOON PHASES

The moon and sun both hold immense magickal energy. Just as the seasonal energy changes throughout the cycles of the sun, so the lunar energy changes depending on the phase of the moon.

New Moon: The new moon is associated with the mysteries of death and rebirth. This is a great time for spellwork involving changes in your life or career, deep meditations, divination, past life regression, contacting spirits, and protection.

Waxing: When the moon is waxing, or growing larger in the sky, its energies can be used for any spells involving increase or gain, such as with money or love. This is a great time for starting new projects, relationships, or setting new goals. The waxing moon is associated with the Maiden aspect of the Triple Goddess.

Full Moon: The full moon is bursting with magickal energy. Many Witches hold their monthly circles at this time in order to harness this powerful energy. It is a great time for spells and rituals of any kind, particularly those involving growth, prosperity, success, healing, and divination. The full moon is associated with the Mother aspect of the Triple Goddess.

Waning: As the moon's light shrinks in the sky, spells involving decreasing or banishing are particularly effective. Rituals for purification, cleansing, releasing negative energy, breaking bad habits, and removing obstacles work well at this time. The waning moon is associated with the Crone aspect of the Triple Goddess.

Although the phase of the moon is something to take into consideration when planning spells and rituals, remember that these correspondences, like wands and athames, are simply tools to help you in your work. If you are really in need of a particular spell, but the moon isn't in the correct position, don't let that stop you. Working with the phases of the moon can help, but it's not a requirement.

DAYS OF THE WEEK

Each day of the week has its own particular energy that can be harnessed and used in spellwork.

Sunday: Success, fame, achievement, prosperity, wealth, promotion, and personal growth

Monday: Women's mysteries, fertility, glamours, emotions, psychic abilities, prophetic dreams, lunar work, sleep, peace, and travel

Tuesday: Courage, bravery, victory, strength, justice and legal matters, defense, and strength

Wednesday: Communication, intelligence, creativity, inspiration, wisdom, luck, writing, music, and the arts

Thursday: Prosperity, abundance, wealth, and healing

Friday: Love, passion, romance, beauty, happiness, harmony, friendship, fertility, pregnancy, and birth

Saturday: Protection, banishing, and cleansing

Just as with the moon phases, if you need a particular spell now, don't feel that you must wait days until you can cast it. Work with the energies of the days if you are able to, but don't let it stop you from performing spells and rituals when you need them.

The most important part of magick is YOU. Your intentions and focus are still the most important elements in any spell or ritual.

ONE LAST THING...

Thank you for reading *Wicca: A Beginner's Guide to Witchcraft, Spells, Rituals, and Magick*! If you enjoyed this book, I'd be very grateful if you'd post a short review at your favorite retailer or book review site. Your support really does make a difference and I read each and every review so I can get your feedback and make my books even better.

Thanks again for your support!

Power Stone

There are various legends in a genuine stone. For your information, the meaning of a part of power stone is introduced.

IOLITE — It is said to brace oneself and refresh one's mind when there are waves of emotions.

AQUA AURA — Gives inspirations and insight. Helps and gives power to fulfill dreams.

AQUAMARINE — It is said to heal sad feelings and stabilizes one's minds. Gives people gentle and pure mind.

APATITE — Washes away the unnecessary in the mind and body. Provides new strength and motivation.

AVENTURINE — Promotes peace, brings out the charm of the owner and gives good health. Great for a women in her pregnancy.

AMAZONITE — Stabilizes and vitalizes the mind. Strengthens thought and inspiration. Indicates the correct path to follow.

AMETHYST — Balances emotions and increases intuition. Cultivate bonds between loved ones and brings out the charm of the owner.

ARAGONITE — Increases sociability, love and affection. It is said to provide one with the power to live a meaningful life.

AMBER — The amulet for longevity. Originally tree sap from the time of dinosaurs, this fossil has been used as a charm for safe birth. Also, it is said to have powers for a good fortune.

EMERALD — It is said to have high healing powers to relieve pain. This stone has deep ties with humans from ancient times.

ELESTIAL — It is said to open unknown doors and lead one to the correct path to follow in times of important decisions.

ONYX — It is said to have the power to arise instinct and stimulate athletic abilities. The stone for driving out evil spirits.

OBSIDIAN — It is said to blossom dormant talent. In ancient times it was used as arrowheads and blades.

GARDEN QUARTZ — From the magical effect it has, it is said to fulfill ones dream and balance minds and emotions. Its mystical appearance is highly attractive.

GARNET — It is said to give the power to courageously fly out and leads persistent efforts to success.

CARNELIAN — Nurtures aspiration and power not to be easily affected by surroundings. Brings out the owner's real strength. It also is an amulet for fertility.

KYANITE — It is said to increase power in thinking and decision making. Also provides power to eliminate dependency.

GREEN GARNET — It is said to have beauty and anti aging powers connecting to new encounters and romances.

CRYSTAL — Cleanses and purifies everything and brings out the power of dormant abilities. It has big powers to absorb the evil.

CHRYSOCOLLA — Cleanses and purifies the aura. This stone gives protection and the power "to detect" for ones who are wishing to get married. Also good for women in her pregnancy.

GREEN TIGER EYE — It is said to release stress mainly from work and vitalize oneself. Gives energy and cleanse the mind and body.

GREEN AGATE — It is said to calm the mind, deepen bonds with close people and lead one to happiness. Brings out one's charm and maintains beauty and health.

KUNZITE — It is said to keep the mind calm and makes one feel the sensation of giving love and affection. Nurtures and cultivates generosity.

CORAL — Harmonizes the nerves and is said to be the amulet for health by balancing the body. Great for gifts for women in her pregnancy.

GOLDEN AURA — It is said to bring out one's talent and charm.

SUNSTONE — It is said to lead the game to a favorable situation and give the power to win against a rival.

SARDONYX — The amulet for matrimonial harmony which stabilizes relationships between families and lovers. It is also said to have powers to draw together good friendships.

SAPPHIRE — It is said to stop confusion and balance the mental and physical body. Gives wisdom and soothes the spirit.

JADE — Blocks bad luck and curses. Protects oneself and their family and is also said to bring in good luck.

CITRINE — Eases stress from interpersonal relationships from work, family and romances. It is also said to have effect on one's fortune.

SUGILITE — Symbol for eternal love and said to make all things go well. One of the three major healing stones of the world.

SMOKY QUARTZ — Gives power to fulfill dreams for people who are inclined to escape from reality. Stimulates goal achievement.

SODALITE — Said to cultivate the necessary power to fulfil one's dreams. Great for people lacking strong will and ability for continuing things. Amulet for studying and dieting.

TURQUOISE — Loved by people from ancient times as an amulet stone. It is said to nurture strong will and strong mind to overcome challenges.

TIGER EYE — Nurtures insight and determination and is a stone for fortune that guides one to success. It is also said to recover eyesight.

CHAROITE — This stone is recommended when the mind and spirit needs to be improved in times such as organizing relationships, overcoming anxiety after change in career or residence. One of the world's three major healing stones.

EYE AGATE — It holds unlimited possibilities to fulfill ones dreams. It is said to lead all to success and has powerful effects in driving out evil spirits.

TOURMALINE — Increases sensitivity and comprehension. Throws out the unnecessary out and vitalizes the physical body. Releases negative ions to relieve excessive stress.

PYRITE — The stone that seizes significant turning points in life. It is said to have powers for everything to go well and to protect one's fortune.

BLACK ONYX — Said to maintain the mind and body in good balance, control confusion in the mind and aid one to become rational.

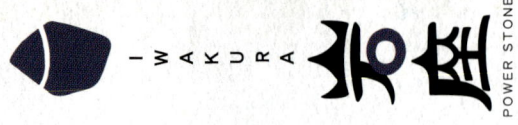
ROSE QUARTZ — For those who wish to bring in romance in their lives. Brings out the beauty of women and nurtures the gentleness she originally has.

ROSE TIGER EYE — It is said to have the power to create bonds and harmonious relationships between people. Also said to fulfill romances and good for women who work.

RHODOCHROSITE — It is said to guide one in a good direction for matters concerning love, for example bringing ones partner for life into their lives. Highly recommended for women.

RHODONITE — Brings gentleness, leverage and love into action. An amulet for amending and deepening relationships.

There are also goods which do not have handling in part by time etc.

How to choose a genuine stone

There are many different interpretations for the meanings and properties of the stones. We have introduced some for your reference and personal enjoyment.

Cleansing method

Crystals

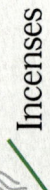

Crystals have a very strong cleansing effect. Crystals will clear the negative energy from other stones and will bring out the essential power it initially has. Put the stone on a large clear crystal cluster or a bag of crystal chips for about 1 to 3 days.

Incenses

One can cleanse their stone from the smoke of burning incenses or white sage. Make sure the smoke spreads throughout all parts of the stone. White sage has an especially remarkable cleansing effect and is said that it will purify the room itself the cleansing is taking place.

BLACK RUTILATED QUARTZ — Increases the passion and spirit for work and naturally guides to an advantageous direction. It is said to increase gambling and fighting luck.

BLUE TIGER EYE — Gives one the power to look into the future and make fortunes. Also provides one with leadership.

BLUE LACE AGATE — Brings tranquility and purity to the mind. It is also said to provide one with fortune, health and many friends.

FLUORITE — It is said it has the power to purify everything. Guides the spirit to a higher level and increases memory skills. Great for students preparing for examination.

HEMATITE — It is said that it helps to clear one's mind and strengthen mental strength. Some have magnetic power which gives better blood flow and purifies the inner body.

PERIDOT — The stone that has been recognized as the "symbol of the sun". Drives off evil spirits and gives wisdom.

WHITE TIGER EYE — Nurtures insight, guides one to success and drives off evil spirits. Good for maintaining one's fortune.

WHITE HOWLITE — The stone that strengthens one's body functions and strengthen overall level of mind and body. Fills one's heart with gentleness and said to give good sleep.

MOTHER OF PEARL — It is said the mother of pearl heals the wounded heart motherly and gently. It brings out the dormant talent, stabilizes the mind and spirit and brings tranquility to the owner.

MALACHITE — It has the power to protect the physical body and drive away evil intentions of others. It is said to break into pieces and substitutes for the owner when the owner is in danger. It also has powers to heal ones heart.

METEORITE — This stone is said to receive information from outer space. It is said to increase one's spirituality and strong mind.

MOLDAVITE — It brings extreme vitality and harmony for one who has been suffering. It also is said to heal the wounds of past traumas.

LAPIS LAZULI — A sacred stone that eliminates evil, fear, jealousy and brings in good luck and success. It has been venerated and loved from ancient times.

LABRADORITE — Vitalizes the inner body and brings vigor to the mind and body.

LARIMAR — It is said to be the symbol for love and peace and brings love and peace to the heart. One of the world's three major healing stones. It is said to have beauty, dieting and anti-aging effects.

RUTILATED QUARTZ — This quartz carries extremely high powers in fortune. It is said to bring confidence and determination and exert power to forward projects.

RUBY — It protects one from any misfortune and is said that its powers can be exerted in any situation such as love, work and exams. It nurtures the passionate mind.

RUBY in ZOISITE — Contains the power of the ying yang. Vitalizes the energy and at the same time heals to remove extra strain on the owner.

RAINBOW MOONSTONE — Brings deep love and peace. Cultures relationship between loved ones. It is said to have the power to create peaceful emotions.

RED TIGER EYE — It is said to have the power to settle common troubles in time of seeking fortune. Also gives vitality to the physical body.

MORE BOOKS BY CASSANDRA LARSEN

Simple Witchcraft Series

Wicca: A Beginner's Guide to Witchcraft, Spells, Rituals, and Magick

Simple Candle Magick: Easy, Powerful Candle Spells for Beginners to Wicca and Witchcraft

The Witches Circle Fantasy Series

Silent Circle

Deceitful Circle

Gray's Dilemma

ABOUT THE AUTHOR

Cassandra Larsen graduated from The College of New Jersey with a degree in English Education. An avid reader of urban fantasy and paranormal romance, she has been dreaming up stories from a very early age. She is the author of the young adult fantasy series *The Witches Circle*. As a practitioner of Wicca for over a decade, she has published a non-fiction series, *Simple Witchcraft*, to help guide beginners in the craft. She lives in Maryland with her husband and two children.

For all the latest news and updates, visit her website at https://larsenbooks.wordpress.com/ or on Facebook at https://www.facebook.com/CassandraLarsenBooks or follow her on Twitter @LarsenBooks

If you Enjoyed this Book, Check Out

Simple Candle Magick!

Candle magick is a fast, easy way to create positive change in your life. In *Simple Candle Magick*, you will find simple, yet powerful spells that are easy to follow and don't require fancy or expensive tools. All you need is yourself and a candle!

These spells are specifically designed for beginners, with easy to follow instructions to guide you through spells for protection, prosperity, healing, study, breaking bad habits, attracting new friends, love, prophetic dreams, and more!

For those that are looking for more advanced candle spell techniques, these spells also includes optional oils and runes that you can add once you become comfortable with the basics. There is even a bonus correspondence guide for the magickal uses of color, runes, and oils to help you create your own personal candle spells simply and easily!

This guide has everything you need to begin practicing candle magick today!

CPSIA information can be obtained
at www.ICGtesting.com
Printed in the USA
LVOW10s1558240418
574671LV00032B/864/P